You Country As Hell Joke Book

Carlos Kane Young

ISBN 978-0-5783-7066-8

Copyright © 2022 by Carlos Kane Young

All rights reserved, including the right of reproduction in any form, or by any mechanical or electronic means including photocopying or recording, or by any information storage or retrieval system, in whole or in part in any form, and in any case not without the written permission of the author and publisher.

Published February 2022

Hello!

My name is Carlos Kane, I am an author, singer-songwriter, and public figure based out of Memphis, TN, and down here in the south we do and say things differently from everyone else. The way we pronounce certain words, talk, walk, joke, and use home remedies will have your sides hurting with laughter. This book wasn't written to offend anyone; it's a book that will bring laughter and great memories to you and yours, so buckle up for 32 pages of straight country fun.

NOTE

YCAH = You Country As Hell

If you eat potted meat and crackers

YCAH

If you cut the mold off a block of cheese and say it's still good

YCAH

If you eat chocolate gravy

YCAH

If you eat chitlins

YCAH

If you eat sauerkraut on hotdogs

YCAH

If you mix cornbread and sugar in pinto beans

YCAH

If you eat oxtails

YCAH

If you put sugar on grits

YCAH

If you reuse your bacon grease

YCAH

If you eat liver mush

YCAH

If you put the oven on to warm up your house

YCAH

If you put a towel under your living room door to keep the cold air out

YCAH

If you save your sauce packets in the kitchen drawer

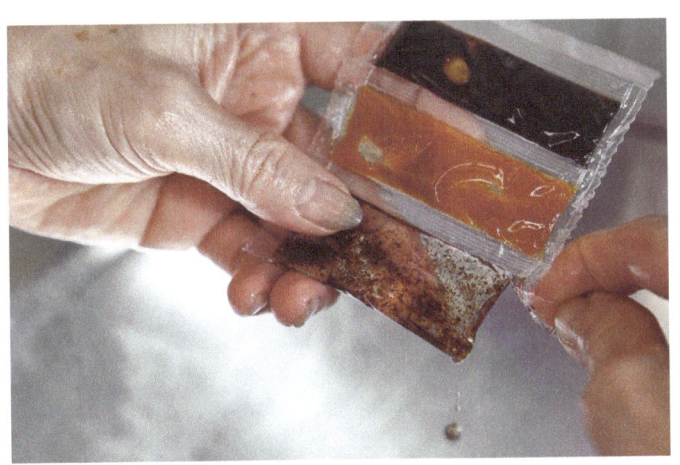

YCAH

If you hang pictures over your living room couch

YCAH

If you wash your clothes in the kitchen sink by hand

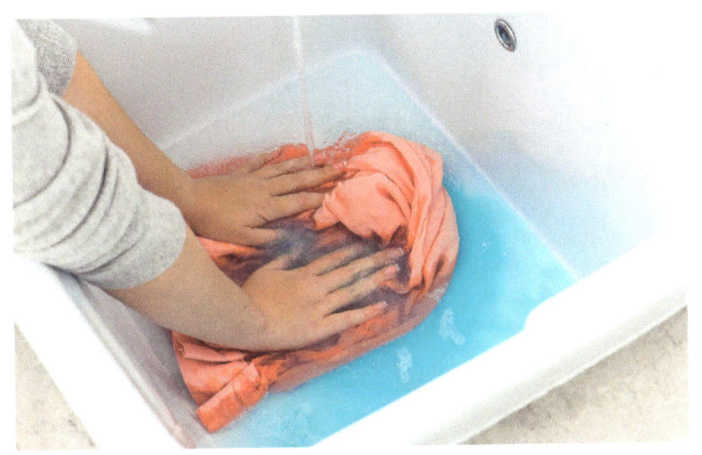

YCAH

If you light your cigarette on the oven burners

YCAH

If you pee behind a tree

YCAH

If you raise your cat and dog together

YCAH

If you use a mattress for a trampoline

YCAH

If somebody knocks on your door and you peep out your blinds to see who it is

YCAH

If you call your granddad "papaw"

YCAH

If you say you're "fixin' to do something"

YCAH

If you say "pop" instead of soda

YCAH

If you say "wranslin'" instead of wrestling

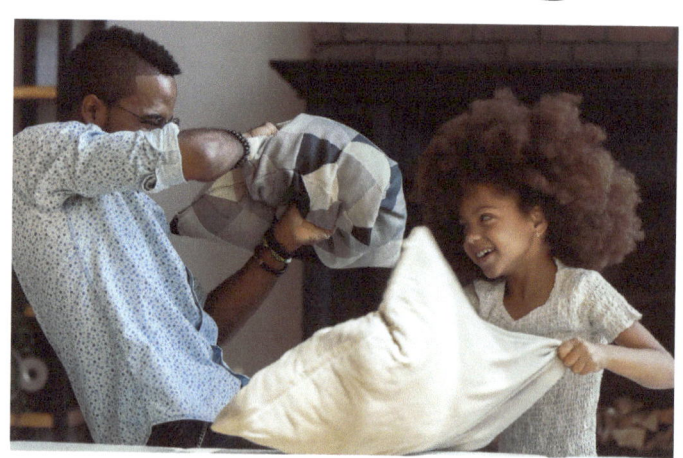

YCAH

If you say "I got to tinkle" instead of pee

YCAH

If you say "over yonder" instead of over there

YCAH

If you say "Mac Donald's" instead of McDonald's

YCAH

If you say "'ghetti" instead of spaghetti

YCAH

If you say "pecann" instead of pecan

YCAH

If you say "warsh" instead of wash

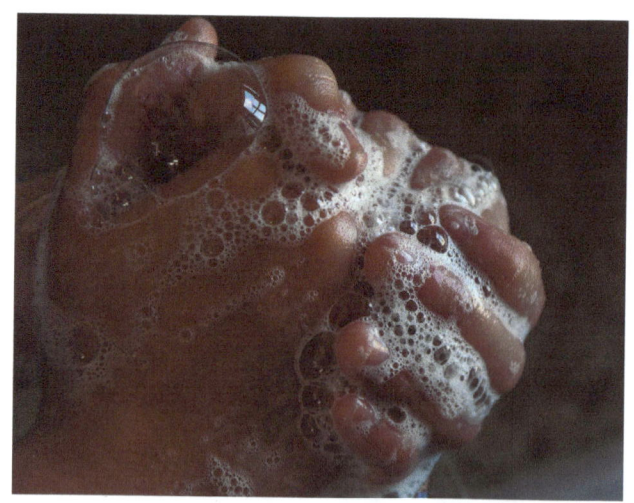

YCAH

If you say "nanna" instead of grandma

YCAH

If you're reading this book I wanna thank you from the bottom of my heart. I know times have been really hard since the pandemic hit and funds are tight for some people, but you guys made it possible to support me. My promise to you is to keep making you laugh through my social media platforms and remaining humble no matter what blessings comes my way. Thank you!

Please follow me: Tiktok: @ckanetriplethreat - Facebook: @carloskane IG: @ckane1975

Believe!

www.ingramcontent.com/pod-product-compliance
Lightning Source LLC
Chambersburg PA
CBHW042044290426
44109CB00001B/32